The Successes of MARCUS GARVEY

written by Akua Agusi

BLACK STAR LINE

THE LAUNCHING OF THE BLACK STAR LINE WILL BE A REAL MESSAGE OF HOPE TO THE NEGRO RACE

The Black Man Must Depend Upon Himself — We Need Factories, Mines, Farms, Ships, Stores, Mills, Colleges and Fisheries.

Illustrated by Kofi Johnson for Afrikom Media Group

FORWARD

This book by Queen Akua fills a very significant void in the rich tradition of African children's literature. Although this is not the first children's book that includes the Honorable Marcus Garvey in it's subject matter, it is one of the very best attempts that I have seen, as a school psychologist and educator, to take the tremendous relevance that the Honorable Marcus Garvey's work has within our revolutionary heritage and make it comprehensible to our young children. The psychological reconstruction of African people must begin within the minds of our young. If we are to reclaim our ancient glory then the proper education of our children is critical towards this end. So many African people have come into the consciousness of who they are only after graduating from high school. Cognitively speaking, this is not the most optimal time period for impressing upon the young subconscious mind the types of information and images necessary for right thinking. The primary years of development and schooling are central to the proper mental programming that African children need in order to be the innovative thinkers of the future. Images, like almost all other forms of information, grow more robust the sooner they are imbedded into the mind. The great neurological leap forward that our children's brains will take between birth and middle school demands that we nourish them with the proper forms of imagery and cultural knowledge. History has taught us well that people are often enslaved by the images and information that surrounds them. African children have been allowed to fall victim to mis-information in the form of Europeanized visual imagery and other aspects of cultural imperialism. Our war for the reclamation of the African mind demands that we surround our young people with rich and powerful images and information from their past. What Queen Akua has done with this book on the life and legacy of arguably the greatest African leader of the 20th century, is in many ways a stroke of genius, as she have effectively taken the complicated and multi-faceted nature of Garvey and Garveyism and made it not only interesting for our children, but stunningly effective in its delivery of content and imagery. Make no mistake, the richly melanated photos that accompany our Sister's literary work serves as the perfect context for imparting the story of such an important movement in the history of African people. African children, around the world, are being socialized and educated on a diet of anti-African imagery which serves as a rich conduit for the teaching of White Supremacy. To reverse this trend of culture worship we have to provide them with an even stronger diet of powerful African imagery. When asked by parents and educators what are some of the most important goals of primary education for African children, included on my list is the need to ensure that our children see beauty and power in the phenotype and experience of African people. Even more important than learning to read is learning to respect one's self; however, it is difficult to respect oneself when you are never shown visually in a positive light. This book on Marcus Garvey not only shows one of our greatest freedom fighters in a positive light, but does so with the strategic use of animation by our brother Kofi, which renders the entire story of the Original Marcus Garvey Movement in a format that is familiar and favorable to our developing young minds. This is a must read for all African children, and the wisdom can also be shared with parents who are unfamiliar with the accomplishments of his Excellency, The Honorable Marcus Mosiah Garvey. I strongly recommend that this book be included on the shelves of every public library and educational institution around the world.

Sincerely,

Dr. Umar Johnson, Psy.D., NCSP, M.Ed.

Doctor of Clinical Psychology & Certified School Psychologist

The Successes of
MARCUS GARVEY

Written by: Akua Agusi

Actual Photo Of Marcus Garvey

Publishing by S.E.E.D.S Publishing.

For information regarding permission, write to S.E.E.D.S Publishing Attention:

Permissions Department, P.O Box 1247 Long Beach CA, 90801.

LIBRARY OF CONGRESS CATOLOGING - IN - PUBLICATION DATA
Agusi, Akua - The Successes Of Marcus Garvey
[1. biography-Non fiction 2. Black History-Non fiction]
Summary: Biography of Marcus Garvey.
Library of Congress Control Number: 2012933235
10 digit ISBN 1-4675-1680-5
13 digit ISBN 9781467516808
Printed in USA

Dedication

This book is dedicated to my Sun Samari. Your mommy loves your spirit. Thank you for being my inspiration. I'm so proud of the Man you will one day grow in to!

I received lots of Love and support from my Community to publish this book. I give thanks to you all!

Special thanks to: Chairman Omali Yeshitela, Dr Umar Johnson, A'Lelia Bundles, Sticman (Of DeadPrez), Dr. Samori Camara, Director at Kamali Academy, Jason Stubbs, Jerry Brown, Cynthia Gordy, Chris Niemoeller, Theresa Whitfield and Kofi Johnson, and the Marcus Garvey Academy for your book reviews and support!

Always with LOVE,
Akua

Everyone is born with a divine purpose. Some people's purpose finds them while others have to seek theirs. In the case of Marcus Garvey, his mother had a feeling very early that her son would accomplish great things. For this reason she gave him the middle name Mosiah! Mrs. Garvey's intuition was correct! Marcus lived to become an incredible fearless leader. He toured the world teaching Black people to be proud of their heritage, encouraged them to be entrepreneurs as well as unite and create a strong Afrikan nation around the globe!

Marcus was born into this world on August 17th 1887 in the small town of St. Ann's Bay, Jamaica. He was the youngest of eleven children. Marcus's father worked as a stone mason, someone who creates things out of cut stone. Marcus's father also had a natural love of books! He loved to read. At times he would stay in a room and read all day long. It is believed that Marcus learned to love books too because of his father.

Marcus's love of reading made him quite the scholar. He would often challenge other children to choose words out of the dictionary for him to spell just for fun! His favorite books were about Jamaican slave revolts. A slave revolt is when slaves would stand up against the people enslaving them and take their freedom. To Marcus these people were heroes!

It was when Marcus was a child that he first encountered racism. His best friend at the time was a white girl from Europe. As they got older, the girl's father told her that she could no longer be friends with Marcus because he was black. That really offended Marcus because he knew that he had been a good friend to her and that being black was not a bad thing at all.

When Marcus was twelve years old his life became really difficult. He lost his father and nine of his ten brothers and sisters. Marcus was left with one sister, Indiana, and his mother.

After the loss of his father and his siblings, his family, much like many others during this time period, did not have much money. Marcus was forced to get a job when he was fourteen years old to help take care of his family. Marcus got a job in a popular city called Kingston, which is the capital city of Jamaica. He worked at a print shop where they made magazines and books.

Two years later Marcus started another job at a newspaper printing company. He was always trying to better himself, so while working there, he began learning at least four new vocabulary words a day.

Marcus would write sentences using the new words to make sure that he remembered them and their meaning. He also began reading the newspapers. He often read in the Jamaican newspapers about other poor people in his country and realized that his family was not the only one that was struggling. When he would walk home from work he began to notice all the people that had tattered clothes, no food to eat, and broken down homes. This began to make him feel very disappointed and upset.

Marcus decided to move to Costa Rica in South America, where people were moving to work in banana plantations. He traveled through many areas of South America, but still all he could find were more poor people of color! Marcus was very confused as to why the people were so poor. It was during this time that he learned about slavery and how it effected African people's history.

He learned that during times of slavery that millions of Afrikan people were kidnapped and shipped all over the world for money. White slave owners would break up families and beat slaves for speaking their native language, partly because the white people did not know the language and didn't want the Afrikan's to speak to one another and come up with a way to revolt. The slave owners would also not allow Afrikans to practice the many different rituals of their culture. One of the only things that Afrikans were allowed to do was dance, and that was just to entertain other white slave owners or guests of the plantation. He discovered that when slavery ended, people were mostly taken from West Afrika, were now living in other countries like Jamaica, the Caribbean islands, the United States of America, South America and Europe. He also discovered that they were living in poverty! Many of the Afrikans had not been allowed to learn to read during slavery. Because of this they were only able to get jobs similar to the work they had done on the slave plantations. This made it very difficult for the Afrikan population to advance in society or even take care of their families. He was outraged!

The more he learned the more distraught he became, so he committed himself to focusing on a solution. He read a book written by a famous black author named Booker T. Washington, which was entitled, "Up from Slavery." This book gave Marcus the inspiration and motivation to want to make a difference and become a leader for his Black Afrikan people.

Marcus returned to Jamaica and shared what he learned, but wasn't able to get enough people together. So Marcus made a plan. He was going to get a huge group of Afrikan people together from all over the world and unite them. He felt as one they would have more power and resources. No matter where on the planet a Black person lived, this organization's sole purpose would be to improve life for them.

In 1914, Marcus organized the U.N.I.A, which stands for:
U. Universal
N. Negro
I. Improvement
A. Association

*During this time period black people or Africans were called 'Negroes.'
(Negro is a word in Spanish that means black.)

Marcus had one of his first speeches at a church with about one hundred people listening. When he walked to the podium and saw all the people in the audience he felt very shocked and scared! He got so nervous he actually fell! He got so embarrassed that he rushed out of the church.

Marcus went home and practiced. He went to listen to other peoples speeches to become more confident. He was determined, next time he would do better!

In 1916 Marcus arrived in New York after traveling throughout the United States looking for U.N.I.A supporters. By 1919 the U.N.I.A had over 100,000 members and Marcus Garvey finally got his second chance to give a speech in front of a large crowd in a popular church. This time he was ready! He had been practicing and now had the courage he lacked the first time. Marcus successfully delivered his speech and the people cheered! He gained an additional 2000 members within weeks!

Marcus came to find that a lot of the hardships that Afrikans were experiencing in the other countries he had visited were also happening in the U.S.A. He also learned that a lot of the black soldiers that had recently returned from war in Europe were now back in New York and very upset. While the soldiers were fighting the war in Europe, they were treated with a level of humanity and respect. However, after returning home, they were greeted with the same issues of discrimination and unfair treatment that they had left years earlier! The soldiers were met with new rules called "Jim Crow Laws" that meant black people could not share facilities with white people, such as restaurants, bathrooms and schools. This prompted many of the ex-soldiers to join the U.N.I.A, feeling comfort in Marcus Garvey's mission of unity for the Afrikan mankind!

Marcus &
Amy Garvey

The Indispensable Weekly
The Voice of the Awakened Negro—The Positive Race

THE

Negro World

Guaranteed Circulation 50,000
Reaching the Mass of Negroes Throughout the World

A Newspaper Devoted Solely to the Interests of the Negro Race

VOL. X. No. 7   NEW YORK, SATURDAY, FEBRUARY 19, 1921

AFRICA THE LAND OF HOPE AND PROMISE
FOR NEGRO PEOPLES OF THE WORLD

Marcus & Amy Garvey

Patronize Your Own Industries!

Fellow Members of the Negro Race:

Why not support your own industries and help to find employment for your Race?

UNIVERSAL STEAM LAUNDRY
62 West 142nd Street

UNIVERSAL TAILORING AND DRESSMAKING DEPARTMENT
62 West 142nd Street

UNIVERSAL NEGRO IMPROVEMENT ASSOCIATION'S PUBLISHING AND PRINTING HOUSE

UNIVERSAL NEGRO IMPROVEMENT ASSOCIATION'S GROCERY

UNIVERSAL NEGRO IMPROVEMENT ASSOCIATION'S RESTAURANT

The year 1919 also saw more progress for Marcus; He married a woman named Amy that he had loved for a very longtime. They wrote many love letters back and forth from Jamaica. Amy even saved his life by throwing herself in front of an armed man that wanted to shoot Marcus Garvey, thankfully she and Marcus were okay! They made a great team. Amy assisted him with both U.N.I.A and the newspaper he started. It was a weekly newspaper called "Negro World." In his paper he included a lot of the information that he gave during meetings and speeches. The newspaper was another tool used to encourage Black people, and because it reached so many people, he could keep everyone informed of issues that faced Afrikan people. By now Marcus Garvey had become an infamous leader!

Official U.N.I.A. Photo

Marcus Garvey held the very first U.N.I.A gathering in Harlem, New York. It began with a grand parade with lots of women and men marching down Lenox Avenue. They were shouting, singing and holding U.N.I.A signs. After the parade, Marcus gave a speech with close to twenty-five thousand people listening; Marcus had conquered his fear of speaking in public.

He said things like:
"Up you mighty race and accomplish what you will".
Which means be proud of who you are and you can do ANYTHING you set your mind to!
He also started the signature saying:
"One God, One Aim, And One Destiny".

During that time a lot of people felt ashamed to be black because they didn't believe they had a reason to feel proud. They believed that all black people were poor; they didn't know much about the Black kings, queens and warriors of Afrika. They had no idea of the rich culture they once possessed while practicing their own culture in Afrika. Marcus Garvey reminded them that they should learn about the history and culture of their Afrikan people and feel proud. No one should feel ashamed of who they are!

The people loved his speech and many signed up for the U.N.I.A
that very same day. Over time there were thousands of U.N.I.A offices
in over 40 countries all over the world!

The largest branches were in parts of the United States, such as Los Angeles, Chicago and New York. There were also offices in South America, Jamaica and even Afrika.

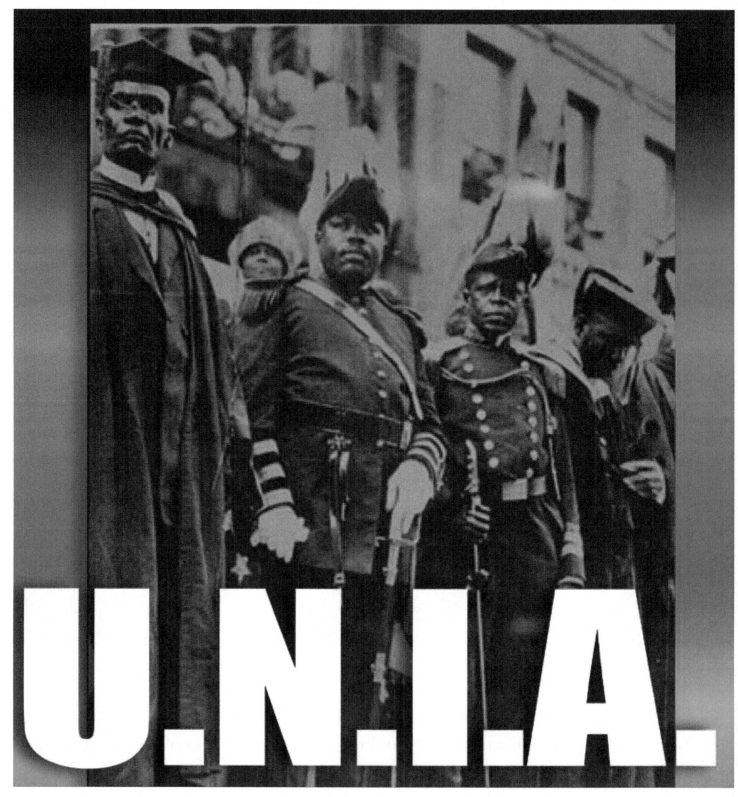

U.N.I.A.

The U.N.I.A was one of the first groups of black people to own their own businesses. In the early 1900's most black people had jobs that required very hard labor for little money. This put great strains on families because often the mother and father would be out working all day leaving little time for their children or each other. Another problem was that almost every "colored" facility was broken down, dirty and below reasonable standard for use.

The U.N.I.A resolved these issues. They gave jobs and opportunities to many black people. They created and owned black restaurants and schools. In the schools the teachers taught with love and taught the children to be proud of where they come from. There were many different businesses including a steam laundry service, two restaurants and three grocery stores. This was a GREAT accomplishment!

There were also U.N.I.A solders to help protect people as well. They had fancy uniforms and they stood very proud. They also had their very own nurses that were called "The Black Cross Nurses" who wore crisp black or white dresses with little hats to match.

Black Star Line Stock Certificate

U.N.I.A. Head Quarters

U.N.I.A. Black Cross Head Quarters

Black Star Line Ship

THE M/V LAKE BOSOMTWE ON HER MAIDEN VOYAGE TO THE PORT OF NEW YORK

OWNED BY: **BLACK STAR LINE LTD.**

HEAD OFFICE:

BLACK STAR LINE LTD.
28th FEBRUARY ROAD
P. O. Box 2760
ACCRA, GHANA

LONDON OFFICE:

AUDREY HOUSE ANNEX
3/4 HOUNDSDITCH
LONDON, E.C. 3.

NEW YORK OFFICE:

BLACK STAR LINE LTD.
42 BROADWAY
NEW YORK 4, NEW YORK

REGULAR

FREIGHT & PASSENGER

SERVICES TO AND FROM

WEST AFRICA

AND

U.K. AND CONTINENT

THE

MEDITERRANEAN

U.S.A. AND CANADA

And

Elsewhere

Members of the U.N.I.A. even went so far as to create their own shipping line called

"THE BLACK STAR SHIPPING LINE"

Each member gave five dollars towards to the cost of buying a huge ship, called the 'SS Fredrick Douglass.' The shipping line would go on to eventually own three ships all owned and operated by U.N.I.A members. The ships made it possible to travel comfortably and trade between Afrika, the Caribbean, Central America, and the United States.

Marcus Garvey, in his continued attempt to unite Black people all over the world, created a flag that would become a national Afrikan symbol that we still see today.

The flag is RED, BLACK, and GREEN and looks like this:

The RED is for blood of the people.

The BLACK is for the people.

The GREEN is for the land.

25

A huge convention in New York at Madison Square Garden was held among all the black leaders of that time called, "The International Convention of the Negro People of the World." During this convention, people flew this flag on their cars as they attended meetings. The convention lasted a month while at the meetings they discussed ways to impove the conditions that Black Afrikans were living in all over the world!

Marcus even started a movement for the liberation of Africa, called "Afrika for the Afrikans." It was started because a lot of Europeans moved to Afrika and took over the Afrikan governments and treated the Afrikan people very unfairly. Garvey suggested that Black people from all over the world move back to Afrika and help redistribute the power to the people in which it belonged. Many countries have taken advantage of the resources and people of Afrika rather than trade fairly or buy materials.

It was also very important to Marcus that Black people learn more about who they truly were. After being in foreign countries for so long, they began to adapt to the traditions and ways of those countries. Black people knew nothing of the beautiful languages they once spoke, the lavish clothing or the purposeful lives and ceremonies practiced in Afrika. Marcus took notice especially in counties like the USA that Afrikans had no desire to know where they came from.

WELCOME

Welcome to Jamaica!

"Garvey"

"Garvey"

"Garvey"

"Garvey"

29

In 1927 Marcus Garvey moved back to Jamaica, where he was treated like the hero he was. He got remarried to a woman named Amy Jacques and had two sons, Marcus Garvey Jr. and Julius Garvey. He ran for government council and won, however things had become so corrupt that it was nearly impossible for Marcus to change things as fast as people wanted.

Marcus Garvey made it his mission in life to help Black people live better lives. He continued his mission until his death on June 10, 1940. He was only 53 years old. His legacy has lived on and to this current day influences people to be great and learn about their history.

There are many great books, posters, statues, parks and streets honoring the great honorable Marcus Garvey. There is even money in Jamaica with Marcus Garvey's face on it. Marcus Garvey encouraged a lot of people to work hard for what they believed in, be very proud of who they were, and to be dedicated in helping other people!

Marcus Mosiah Garvey was once a little boy from a poor family in Jamaica with an idea. With determination and faith, he made a BIG difference in other peoples lives and this world!

31

It is still very important, even today, to continue to learn about your people's history, culture and traditions. You can do this through reading books, using the internet, and learning from other people! Also never be afraid to be the first person to speak up or create a new idea about anything! One person can make a huge difference.

And that one person can be YOU!!!

Color the Honorable Marcus Mosiah Garvey!

Do you remember the colors of the flag?

36

Look for these past and new releases...

"Madam C.J. Walker's Road To Success"

"Saniyah's Face"

"Queen Nzingha The Warrior Queen"

"Haiti's (Ayiti's) Independence"

"Nyilah"

"The Successes Of Black Wallstreet"

"Samari And The G.O.A.T"

More Information at www.AkuaAgusi.com

The Successes of
MARCUS GARVEY

written by Akua Agusi

The true story about Marcus Garvey, a courageous young man who defied great odds to lead and inspire a national movement that changed the minds and lives of millions of people across the world and left a legacy that still continues to encourage people to be great today. After reading this book never again will you question the power of one person or one idea!

$11.00
ISBN 978-1-4675-1680-8
51100>
9 781467 516808

CPSIA information can be obtained
at www.ICGtesting.com
Printed in the USA
BVOW07s2152261217
503583BV00006B/42/P

9 781467 516808